Yes I Can

Austin C. Carpenter

To My Son

You are the Apple in Mommy's Eye.

The very existence of you deserves my love, support and encouragement.

May I continue to celebrate you and all of your accomplishments.

As you grow and continue to mature may you dream big and achieve all that God has planned for you.

May your heart and face smile always and be filled with great joy.

May your way be unhindered and your territory be enlarged.

May you rule in righteousness and prosper and have great success in all that you do !

May you always honor and obey God.

May you have long life.

I love you
Mom

Austin and I are so excited that we get to share our 'Yes I Can' story with you and your little one. You will find short but impactful affirmations and/or declarations to speak aloud to your little one while reading. These affirmations/declarations are a reminder of God promises and/or views of your little one.

Our hope is that it will empower your little one to conquer any challenge he or she may face; while creating a 'Yes I Can' mindset.

Austin and I would like to thank you for your support and hope you enjoy the book.

WHEN A TASK SEEMS IMPOSSIBLE TO DO,

I CAN COUNT ON YOU TO FIGURE IT OUT.

It's your turn parent ; please turn and look your little one in the eyes and speak the below statement out loud to them :

For skillful and Godly wisdom shall enter your heart, and knowledge will delight you.

Proverbs 2:10

WHEN YOU ARE AFRAID,

I CAN COUNT ON YOU TO BE BRAVE.

It's your turn parent; please turn and look your little one in the eyes and speak the below statement out loud to them:

No, in all these things we are more than conquerors through him who loved us.

Romans 8:37

WHEN YOU DO NOT KNOW HOW,

I CAN COUNT ON YOU TO ASK FOR HELP.

It's your turn parent; please turn and look your little one in the eyes and speak the below statement out loud to them:

For if you ask you will receive, and if look you will find.

Matt 7:7

WHEN YOU DO NOT LOOK THE SAME AS OTHERS,

I CAN COUNT ON YOU TO KNOW THAT YOU ARE BEAUTIFUL AND PERFECT AND EVERY WAY.

It's your turn parent ; please turn and look your little one in the eyes and speak the below statement out loud to them :

I will praise you, for I am fearfully and wonderfully made; wonderful are your works, and my soul knows it very well.

Ps 139:14

It's your turn parent; please turn and look your little one in the eyes and speak the below statement out loud to them:

You are brave and are my delight.

As you grow older you will have great success and will do well.

God and I care for you and you are always in our hearts.

I love you.

CPSIA information can be obtained
at www.ICGtesting.com
Printed in the USA
LVHW061012041220
672002LV00026B/89